When I Get
to Heaven
the only one
shaking will be
Elvis

When I Get to Heaven the only one shaking will be

Elvis

Jim Jackson

My Battle with Parkinson's

REDEMPTION
PRESS

Published by Redemption Press, PO Box 427, Enumclaw, WA 98022.

ISBN 13: 978-1-63232-401-6
Library of Congress Catalog Card Number: 2005903340

DEDICATION

I dedicate this book to the most important people in my life:

My mother, Bettye, who gave me life.

My wife, Laura, who gave me love.

My daughters, Mary Elizabeth and Sims, who gave me gray hair.

And to the most important person:

Jesus, who gave me eternity.

Special thanks to the following friends:

Tim Irby, for taking such superb pictures, and for putting so much of your time and talents into this book.

Charles Schuchard, my friend, my brother-in-law, and part-time wordsmith. Thanks for always being there with an encouraging word. Your positive comments gave me credibility with the family when everyone thought my writing was a "phase." Your friendship has been a blessing to me.

A special thanks to Oprah, a lady so special that all you need to say is her first name and everyone knows who, you're talking about. Your show with Michael J. Fox, where you spoke with him about how therapeutic writing a book was, gave me the idea to do this. You have inspired many people. God bless you.

TABLE OF CONTENTS

FOREWORD

I chuckle every time I read the title of this book. I based it on my strong faith, knowing that my Lord will remove the baggage that comes along with this disease when I meet Him at the pearly gates of heaven.

This book is my attempt to document my battle with Parkinson's disease, nicknamed "PD." This battle, while deadly serious, is fought by me and my friends and family with prayer and humor. I believe it is important to laugh at yourself and the surprises that PD brings on a daily basis. I do not mean to minimize anyone's personal experiences with this disease. I realize what a horrible illness it is. I just choose to meet this bump in the road of life with a laugh rather than a cry.

This book is a celebration of all the people who have assisted me in this battle. They have made the journey a blessing.

When I Get to Heaven, the Only One Shaking Will Be Elvis

I once told Joe White, a mighty Christian man who is the owner of Kanakuk Kamps, that the Lord blessed me with Parkinson's. Joe responded that not many people would thank the Lord for giving them a disease and that I was a role model to others. That is my goal.

I believe the Lord gave me PD, not to see how I would handle it, but to show others how to handle it. This book is my way of doing that.

I hope you enjoy these tales of the happenings in my life. Don't be afraid to laugh. I guarantee you these incidents resulted in much laughter when they occurred.

May God bless.

—Jim Jackson

Chapter 1

PD SNEAKS INTO MY LIFE

Have I not commanded you? Be strong and courageous. Do not be terrified, do not be discouraged,
for the Lord your God will be with you wherever
you go.

—Deuteronomy 1:9 (NIV)

Parkinson's disease ("PD") came quietly into my life
in the spring of 1996. I am a special agent with the
Criminal Investigation Division of the Internal Revenue
Service. Now, to set your mind at ease, let me assure
you that special agents do not audit income tax returns.
We perform investigations into various types of crimes,
including money laundering and drug dealing.

My agency sends new agents to Glynco, near
Brunswick, Georgia, to be trained by a group of senior
special agents. In 1996, I was assigned to teach senior
special agents advanced money laundering investigation

techniques for four weeks. I was excited, partly because it was a reward for my hard work and also because it gave me the opportunity to work on my golf game.

I had been a fairly good golfer, shooting consistently in the high 70s for eighteen holes. But work and family life had shifted my priorities away from golf, and I was eager to see what I could shoot after some daily practicing.

The second stop I made when I got to St. Simon's Island, my home for the next four weeks, was one of its many beautiful golf courses. I immediately signed up for the practice range membership and gladly paid $200 for the right to hit practice balls all day, seven days a week, for four weeks. I enjoyed my daytime teaching activities, but lived for the late-afternoon and early-evening hours I spent on the range beating golf balls. Whenever I called my wife, Laura, she said I talked like I was in heaven.

Sometime early during the third week, I began to notice that my right arm was often hanging close to my side. It did not swing as naturally as my left arm did, but rather as if it were in a sling. Being a typical man, and since it didn't hurt, I ignored it, hoping it would just go away.

Laura came up with "golf overload" as the likely culprit. I believed her and took a couple of days off from golf.

When my teaching assignment ended, I returned to my Jackson, Tennessee, home with my new best friend, PD, though I did not yet know him by name.

TIDBITS

The four primary symptoms related to Parkinson's are:

a. *Rigidity*—stiffness. Can be experienced in an arm, leg, toes, or fingers. My initial symptom was my right arm hanging close to the body.
b. *Tremors*—shaking or trembling. Usually in one hand or leg, but can be in both.
c. *Dyskinesia*—my nemesis. The slowing down or stopping of the body's movements. This can be caused by some medications.
d. *Loss of Balance*—Be very careful of falls.

IS THERE A DOCTOR IN THE HOUSE?

Back at home, the worry remained with me. My arm didn't hurt, but without specific effort on my part, it hung by my side as if it were broken. I thought I might have had a stroke, but figured if I lost some weight and exercised, I would be good as new. I began the infamous fen-phen diet and lost weight quickly, but I became terribly nervous.

It was early fall, and my extended family back in Oxford, Mississippi, was beginning their annual task of preparing the land and buildings of the deer camp for the upcoming season. This usually includes a couple of "men only" weekends comprised of bush-hogging the deer fields, fire lanes, food plots, and access areas. Grass seed has to be planted and fertilizer applied. These working weekends are always fun, but terribly tiring. That year was no exception.

When I Get to Heaven, the Only One Shaking Will Be Elvis

It was about time to quit on Saturday when my nephew Mike Roberts came up to me and asked if I was OK. I asked why, and he said he noticed that my arm had been shaking. "Everyone's worried about you," he said.

I blew it off as exhaustion, but I don't think I fooled anyone. Not even myself. Soon after returning, I made an appointment to see my doctor.

Dr. David Garey, my family doctor, complimented me on my desire to get in shape, but scolded me for taking the fen-phen drugs. He suggested I get off those drugs immediately and see if losing weight by other means helped my arm.

TIDBITS

Some other signs of PD are:

a. Handwriting becomes smaller. This was one of my first symptoms, but it has now returned to normal.

b. "Parkinson's Face." Some call it "mother-in-law face" because no matter what you do, you can never smile. (My mother-in-law smiles all the time. See picture.)

c. Excessive sweating. I once had to strip down to a T-shirt in late November at a night ball game due to sweating. The temperature was 38 degrees.

d. Inability to sleep or vivid dreaming.

e. Depression. This one worries me the most.

f. A slight tremor in the hand or foot.

g. An overall stiffness in the body.

h. A change in attitude. Being grumpy or difficult to deal with.

About this time, my Bible study group was looking for a new church home. We were leaving our former church due to a disagreement about what was being taught to our children. While I was in Georgia teaching, several of my friends found a new church that was being started in our neighborhood. This church was the same denomination, but was an alternative to the big church in town.

Ministers Brian and Tracy Stewart, a young couple, had been led to Jackson to start a new, conservative church. Their church was less than three miles from our home. We were so happy with our new church and ministers, we were like Christians on steroids!

This began my "arming for battle." Here the Lord was going to supply me with everything I needed to overcome what was about to be placed upon me. My close friends Jerry Dotson and Ben Hall have walked step by step with me throughout this battle.

Sometime in 1996, Jerry, Ben, and I attended a Promise Keepers rally in Memphis. Two days of singing, praying, and preaching by thousands of men blew me away. Men of all colors, denominations, and status sat side by side, praising Jesus. It doesn't get any better than that.

TIDBITS

Many of my friends have said, "I thought PD was a disease that old people get." It is, with the average age of diagnosis being about sixty years old. However, some "young onset" patients begin showing symptoms before the age of fifty.

Early-onset Parkinson's can be overwhelmingly depressing due to the special problems these patients face, such as:

a. Loss of employment
b. Loss of family
c. Sexuality concerns
d. Loss of freedom (unable to drive, travel, etc.)

I knew all these things were happening to me because my Lord loved me, and He was preparing me. Let me tell you what He did next.

THE HOLY SPIRIT VISITS "THE GREAT BANQUET"

In the fall of 1996, a group of eight men from my new church attended a weekend retreat called "The Great Banquet." This had a greater impact on my life than any other single event.

At this retreat, Christian men give their personal testimonies, telling their stories about how they came to know Christ as their personal Lord and Savior. Some of these men had to be knocked in the teeth by the Lord to get their attention; others found God in the shadows of a prison cell. This retreat is also known as "The Walk to Emmaus," "*Cursillo*," and "*Tres Dias*." Though churches often sponsor this weekend, it is nondenominational.

This weekend provides men with a chance to open up about whatever is troubling them and give it all to God for Him to handle. His shoulders are big and He is ready to walk with us, even carry us, throughout our journeys to His kingdom. Surrounded by friends and my new pastor, Brian Stewart, this was a once-in-a-lifetime weekend for me.

During the midst of this experience, PD raised its ugly head. My right arm began to shake, sometimes a little, sometimes a lot. Jerry, who is a nurse, told me it was probably sleep deprivation combined with an overdose of Diet Coke and cookies. At the time I thought he was probably right, since our room contained several loud snorers.

But when my shaking got worse, I took my concerns to the pastor. He said he thought it was the Holy Spirit in my body. As much as I wanted to believe that, I still felt I had a problem lurking somewhere.

At the closing ceremony, I got up to thank the men who had changed my life that weekend. I was shaking like a leaf on a windy day. I said, "I bet you haven't seen a man this big shake so bad since Elvis died." The room erupted in laughter.

TIDBITS

Parkinson's tremors usually begin in one hand, and they have a rhythmic motion. Some people say it looks as if you're playing a guitar. Stress usually causes an increase of the movement.

After attending "The Great Banquet," guests are offered the opportunity to serve as staff on a future team. I had the privilege of serving twice as a table leader and once as a member of the kitchen staff. These banquets provided me with the opportunity to serve my Lord.

At each weekend the Lord answered my prayers by letting me witness to everyone there that PD was not a death sentence. In fact, to a large degree, PD is what you let it be.

Numerous people came up to me and told me how great it was to see me working at that banquet. My reply: "All glory and praise goes to God, for allowing me to let my light shine." I must have said that two hundred times each weekend. Where will you let your "light" shine?

I have many special memories of these banquets. I also learned that I can't reach everyone. At one banquet where I was serving as kitchen help, one of the table leaders came to me and asked if I would talk to a guest at his table. This man had recently been given the news that he had Parkinson's and he was not handling it well.

The table leader didn't have to tell me which guest he was talking about; I could spot him a mile away because his body was moving about so much.

Over the next three days I tried to witness to this guest on dozens of occasions, but with no apparent results. He left the same bitter man who had arrived, blaming the only one who could quiet those movements: God. Perhaps some of the seeds I tried to plant impacted him later, but I don't know for sure.

Not all of your opportunities will be success stories, but none will be failures, because you will grow in your faith as you serve your God. Open up your life to new opportunities to grow in your relationship with God. You will be richer for the experience.

At one of these banquets, when I was serving as a table leader, I met Jeff Hooper through his brother David. David has a great heart for the Lord. And Jeff told me he was deeply moved by the witnessing the men did through the talks at this banquet.

After that weekend our paths did not cross again until we both became involved in the launch of Fellowship Bible Church. Over the past several years we have become close friends. Jeff has blessed my life in many ways.

The Lord has enabled us to witness to a mutual acquaintance of ours, whom I'll call Don. Don grew up in Brownsville, Tennessee. I came to know him in the course of an investigation I was conducting. He was suspected of money laundering.

The moment I met Don, I sensed he was a man of God who had been led astray by the evils of money. I treated him with respect throughout my investigation, and I think he appreciated that. Don was always concerned about my health and what my PD was up to. However, the facts I uncovered in my investigation resulted in Don being sentenced to more than two years in prison.

After Don's final court date, the Brownsville newspaper printed an article that detailed the case against him, including the fact that I was the agent who had worked the investigation. Shortly thereafter, Jeff called me. He said he'd read the article and he told me about his friendship with Don.

Several weeks later Jeff called and said he was going to Arkansas to visit Don in prison. He asked me to go with him. I immediately thought of all the things that made the trip impossible. But I couldn't hang up the phone. Jeff continued talking to me until I agreed to go.

The look on Don's face when he saw that I was one of his visitors revealed absolute shock. But the three of us had a heart-warming visit as we shared Christ's love. I hope Don will allow the Lord to use him to bring his message of "losing it all" and then finding out that he hadn't lost anything of value. Don could be a powerful witness.

Whether you are battling Parkinson's or any other disease or obstacle, your battle will be aided by surrounding yourself with Christian friends.

TIDBITS

If you've been diagnosed with PD, find a good support group. Don't deny your illness. Find the best medical and mental care available to you.

MY COMPANION FINALLY GETS A NAME

I have two beautiful daughters: Sims, who was eight at the time I was diagnosed with PD (1997), and Mary Elizabeth, who had just turned ten. In addition, God had blessed me with Laura, my wife of seventeen years at that time. Laura is the hero of my life.

Everyone who has been afflicted by PD knows the importance of loving, understanding caregivers. They are the ones who put up with the "poor me's" that sometimes sneak into a patient's mind.

Laura was raised with a strong faith. I am grateful to her parents, Mary and Denton Sims, for raising such a complete woman and then trusting me enough to grant me the honor of making her my wife. At no time did Laura ever say that she got a raw deal . . . well, at least not because of the PD. She has met every challenge by attacking it head-on.

After I returned from my first Great Banquet, I was more determined than ever to find out what was wrong with me. I made a beeline back to Dr. Garey. This time he seemed concerned about possible brain problems. I later learned that he was worried I might have a tumor.

Dr. Garey scheduled an appointment with Dr. Joe Rowland, a neurosurgeon with an office in Jackson. I went to see Dr. Rowland in December and found him to be a delightful person and a compassionate physician. He scheduled an MRI of my brain.

I have claustrophobia, so that procedure was akin to being buried alive. I survived the tube, barely, and returned to see Dr. Rowland in early January.

When I Get to Heaven, the Only
One Shaking Will Be Elvis

Dr. Rowland left the room to review the film. He returned with a broad smile. He gave me a big hug and said, "You don't have a tumor. All you have is Parkinson's." He explained that Parkinson's is not a life-threatening disease, though it is a "life-altering disease." I'm grateful to Dr. Rowland for putting PD in its proper perspective.

I must have been chosen by God to carry this banner for Him, because it's rather strange that I should have this disease. The average age of the onset of Parkinson's is sixty[i]. However, 10 to 20 percent of persons with PD develop it before the age of fifty. About half of these are diagnosed before the age of forty.[ii] I was forty-three when I was diagnosed. I turned fifty-one on February 5, 2005.

In addition, as far as we can tell, I am the only one in my immediate family to ever have Parkinson's. One of my wife's grandfathers had it in his eighties.

Parkinson's is not fatal, but it does reduce longevity and quality of life. It is up to the patient to meet it head-on and not let it take total control. Besides, I firmly believe that how long I live is up to God, not a disease.

THE REPORTS OF MY DEATH
ARE GREATLY EXAGGERATED

Soon after my diagnosis, an onslaught of calls began. Now, I don't like having a fuss made over me. After all, a well-respected doctor had just told me that "all" I had was Parkinson's. Yet people were constantly trying to console me on my plight. It was as if the local paper had printed my obituary.

My wife ran into a friend just a few months after I had been diagnosed, and he asked her if I was still working. Several people explained to me in detail what horrible deaths their fathers had gone through with Parkinson's. Some days I would have rather endured a root canal or hemorrhoid surgery than to talk to another "well-wisher."

Don't get me wrong. PD does have its depressing periods. But I've spent worse times in Tiger Stadium in Baton Rouge, watching my Ole Miss Rebels get beat, than I've had fighting PD. The secret is not to let the disease keep you down, but to learn to laugh in its face.

Calls, letters, and visits became a daily trial. I considered it a chore to accept people's condolences without yelling at them that I wasn't dead yet and had no intention of checking out any time soon.

If you have PD, you will have to walk a fine line here. Part of you will want to withdraw from the world and shut the door to society. But this is extremely selfish. You need to let your friends express their feelings. That's a part of the grieving process. By getting this step behind them, you are allowing them to move ahead to the acceptance step, and then the healing step.

I know these friends of mine were just showing that they cared, and I am truly grateful for all of my friends who called, wrote notes, or came by. They meant well, and I know what was in their hearts.

When I Get to Heaven, the Only One Shaking Will Be Elvis

The actions I appreciated most were from two guys I consider my best friends: Jerry Dotson and Bob Kunze. They refused to let me mope around, not even for a minute. Jerry and his wife Jackie, were two of the first people we told that I had PD. Their initial response was, "We can get through this," and they have been there every step of the way. They are not afraid to laugh at something PD does to me. We've had many great laughs at the expense of my disease.

Recently, these two were at my house in the dead of winter, just sitting around chatting. I went outside to get the dogs from their pen and "froze." "Freezing" is when PD robs you of the ability to move. Your mind gets stuck and you can't move until the medicine kicks in or someone comes to assist you.

So I was outside, frozen, while my wife and friends were inside having a blast without me. After about fifteen minutes, my medicine kicked in and I was able to drag myself inside, with the dogs wrapped around me as if I were a maypole.

The first words out of Jackie's mouth were, "Where have you been, dear?"

"Where have I been?" I sputtered. "I've been outside frozen, listening to all of you having a party."

Jerry said, "I thought you were gone a long time."

We laughed for hours. Then we set a time limit for me to be out of the room.

TIDBITS

"Freezing" is caused by dyskinesia, an excess of protein in the body. Dyskinesia can be debilitating, robbing you of your ability to walk or talk.

Bob Kunze has been my best friend for almost twenty years. He has never let me feel sorry for myself. I remember his first phone call after I was diagnosed with Parkinson's.

"Just think of the neat job opportunities you have," Bob said. "You could shake the paint at Sherwin Williams, mix drinks at the bar, or ring the Christmas bell outside Wal-Mart."

Bob and I play in a golf tournament in Little Rock every year, and we've had some unique rounds. Bob plays a mind game that shocks the other golfers in our group, but is great at breaking the tension about my condition. He'll walk up to me just as I begin to tee off and ask, "Hey, Jim, what's shaking? Besides you, of course." Responses range from gasps to laughter.

Bob's welcome humor has kept me in the middle of the road for years.

ARMED AND READY FOR BATTLE

In those first few months after my diagnosis, God surrounded me with Christian friends and a deep hunger to read and study His words found in the Bible. Then He put two great doctors in my life to get me into the right frame of mind.

Chapter 2

THE MIDDLE YEARS

Therefore we do not lose heart. Though outwardly we are wasting away, yet inwardly we are being renewed day by day. For our light and momentary troubles are achieving for us an eternal glory that far outweighs them all. So we fix our eyes not on what is seen, but on what is unseen. For what is seen is temporary, but what is unseen is eternal.

—2 Corinthians 4:16-18

Parkinson's disease, my constant companion, is always there, waiting to raise its ugly head at just the right, or more likely the wrong, moment. Whether it is at work, during an interview, or at a sporting event, PD confuses my words, shuffles my steps, or shakes my body. This has caused varied reactions from people. Most comments are touching, though a few have been downright hateful.

When I Get to Heaven, the Only
One Shaking Will Be Elvis

The stares affect me the most. But people are going to stare, that's all there is to it.

Once, I attended an Ole Miss ball game by myself. I played football from junior high through junior college, and I was always the first to get dressed out for the game. Today, as a fan, I still get to the stadium at least an hour before kickoff.

As fate would have it, just as I got to the stadium that day, PD struck, causing me to walk in short, choppy steps. Three drunks came by and saw me. One said in a loud voice, "Hey, look at him! And I thought I was drunk!"

After that my doctor gave me a card that states, "I am not drunk. I have a condition called Parkinson's disease." Eight years later, I still use that card.

One of the biggest fears many PD patients have is losing their jobs. Fortunately for me, I work for some of the most compassionate individuals in the federal government. The IRS employs fewer than three thousand special agents, and only a few dozen are involved in the undercover area. We are a tight family. These men and women work hard and are rewarded with an excellent reputation in the law enforcement community. I count all of my fellow agents as friends.

Management has also been kind. These men and women lead the finest group of financial investigators in the world. Criminal Investigation agents are always in demand for their abilities to "follow the money." CI management has handled my well-being as a primary concern.

Patrick Shirey is my supervisor in Memphis. His predecessor, Judith Nash, was a super leader, practically a living legend. No one thought her replacement would be able to fill her shoes.

But Patrick, known as Pat to the agents, has stood beside me in all of my battles, both personal and work related. As I write this, I am about two months away from qualifying for full retirement, as opposed to being on disability status.

Many employers are scared to have a worker with a disability. My advice for everyone who has lost a job because of PD is to lean upon our Savior. He will provide you with the answers.

TIDBITS

Studies indicate that 25 to 35 percent of individuals diagnosed with Parkinson's are still actively working.[iii] Parkinson's treats each patient differently. If you are able to work, by all means do so. This shows others that PD does not win every battle.

One of my "freezing" events happened while I was at work. My partner, Kay Frye, and I were making an early trip to Memphis to assist in the execution of search warrants. Knowing it was going to be a long day, I delayed taking my first dose of medicine until we were almost in Memphis. We arrived in Memphis in the early morning, so we stopped at a cafeteria for breakfast. I ate a big bacon biscuit. Afterward, Kay decided to take a restroom break, so I did too.

Just as I was attempting to pull up my pants, PD hit me. My arms became useless and I couldn't move. I just stood there, with my pants around my ankles, my weapon sitting on the back of the toilet.

I figured Kay and I were about to become much closer friends, as she was going to have to help me get dressed. Then I remembered seeing a commercial on television in which people were lying down to put on their pants. Lucky for me, I was the first customer that morning. I would not have wanted to lie down on that floor in the evening.

I was just finishing when the door opened and an elderly man, probably eighty years old, looked in. He saw me lying on the floor, pulling up my pants, with two badges on my shirt and a gun sitting on the back of the toilet. I've never seen a man that age move so fast!

Shortly after that, my medications kicked in. I quickly retrieved my weapon and left the restroom. I still chuckle when I think about what that elderly gentleman must have thought.

TIDBITS

If you experience "freezing," try to relax your muscles. Be patient. Take single large steps, lifting your knees high with each step, or step over somebody else's foot.

Also, examine what you are eating. Protein turned out to be the cause of my freezing.

Ever since I was diagnosed, I think management has been nervous about allowing me to carry a weapon. I suspect they believe they would be negligent in their responsibilities if they didn't watch out for my ability to drive the government car and my ability to handle a weapon properly. You would think that someone with PD wouldn't be able to shoot, but I always qualified in the top one or two, even with the shakes. The other agents thought it strange that I was still an expert shot with those shakes. But when a gun went into my hands, the shaking stopped. I'm not sure if that was because I've been around firearms all my life or because the good Lord knew I had to qualify in order to keep my job. I'm betting He calmed my tremors since I managed to qualify each time I shot.

While I can't say that this doesn't worry me somewhat, I have been able to set it on the "trouble shelf," a place in my mind where I put all the troubles that I can't control. These are the ones I let God handle.

TIDBITS

Maintaining a positive attitude is the most essential element in your battle against Parkinson's. The diagnosis of PD is not a death sentence. It is a message to you and your family that some changes need to be made in your life. Attack these changes with a passion. Don't let the disease win.

I worry about what people are saying about me far more than I should. It feels as though everyone is watching me. Sure, some people watch. But how vain is it to think that the whole world cares about what I'm doing?

Kids are brutally honest, and they'll say whatever is on their minds. Sometimes it doesn't make sense, but you can usually expect to laugh.

OUT OF THE MOUTHS OF BABES

As Art Linkletter often said, "Kids say the darndest things." I have found that to be true, especially when dealing with an old man who's shaking and moving around like his pants are on fire.

Perhaps the sweetest encounter I've had with a young person came when I was watching my older daughter play soccer. Remember, I'm the guy who used to dress out hours before a game just to get pumped up. Well, mix that intensity with my friend PD, and you have what my wife calls a "moving machine."

To say that I move a lot while watching a sporting event would be an understatement. Before my medications were changed, dyskinesia caused me to rock from side to side.

A second-grade girl named Bonna Hardee was also at my daughter's soccer game to watch her sister play, but apparently I was more interesting. Bonna sat behind me and next to my wife, who was her school librarian. After watching me gyrate for about ten minutes, Laura heard Bonna mumbling to herself, "I think he thinks he's in the jungle."

Bonna continued to study me. "He must think he's a monkey."

A few minutes later, Bonna said, "I think he has to go to the bathroom."

Laura told me about Bonna's observations that afternoon. PD did not win the battle that day because we looked it straight in the face and laughed at it.

The Lord, through my two daughters, led me to the Fellowship Bible Church of Jackson. Our family had been floundering at the church we'd helped establish. We loved the congregation, but were unhappy with the lack of a youth group or youth activities.

We had two teenage daughters who needed a youth group, and the youth group at our church consisted of four teenagers, two of which were ours. Laura and I decided we had to do something.

Laura's sister and brother-in-law, Robbie and Charlie Schuchard, introduced us to a nondenominational church in Little Rock, Arkansas, called the Fellowship Bible Church, which stresses the teachings found in the Bible. Our family made several visits to the church and were amazed at how a mega-church could make us feel so at home.

We had also seen great spiritual growth in the Schuchard family since joining that church. Charlie, an ordained elder, had grown weary of the liberal leanings of many of the mainline denominations, and when he was transferred to Little Rock, his family felt they needed to look for a conservative, Bible-believing church. And they found it.

Laura and I discussed moving to Little Rock to attend Fellowship and to surround our children with Christian friends. But the Lord obviously wanted us to stay in Jackson, because as we were setting up a move to Little Rock, one of my dearest friends, John Campbell, came by to see us and asked where we were going to church. We told John about our frustrations, and he invited us to attend the planting of a new church he was helping to establish in Jackson. Laura asked the name of the church, and to our surprise, he said, "Fellowship Bible Church."

We took that as a sign to stay in Jackson. And we have been abundantly blessed in this church. It is led by a leadership team of godly men. And the pastors—Eugene, Randy, Johnathan, and Fred—are truly set apart by God to equip their congregation to go out into the world and lead others to know Christ as their personal Lord and Savior. How important it is, especially in today's society, to belong to a church like Fellowship.

TIDBITS

Here are some helpful tips on how to PD-proof your house.

a. Put handrails up steps, both inside and outside your home. Rails are also helpful along walkways and in bathrooms.

b. Have chairs with sturdy backs and arms, because there are times when you must "flop" into a chair in order to sit. I sometimes use a desk chair with rollers to move about.

c. Carefully go over your path to the bathroom and other places you regularly walk, and remove anything that might cause you to fall. You need a "safe zone" around you.

d. Make sure the areas you are using at night (bedroom and/or bathroom) are well lit. Keep a flashlight handy, as well as a cell phone to make emergency calls if needed.

e. Have a comfortable chair, possibly a recliner, next to your bed in case you wake up in the middle of the night. You'll be surprised how much sleep you can get in that chair!

Jerry Dotson and I make coffee for the church on Sunday mornings every other month. It is served, along with donuts, during the time of fellowship before the service. Our church has been blessed to have an abundance of children, and kids love donuts.

One of my friends at church is Dr. Ray Howard. Ray's son is also named Ray. Little Ray came up to the counter to get a donut, but when he saw me, he backed away. He looked at me with an expression that could best be described as a cross between fear and worry.

I told him I was fine, that I just had a disease called Parkinson's that made me move and shake a lot. He seemed to accept my explanation, as well as a six-year-old can, but continued to act leery of me.

After church one day, little Ray came up to me, looked me in the eye, and asked, "Can you catch it?"

He hadn't been afraid of me. He was just scared that he might catch my illness.

TIDBITS

Parkinson's is not contagious, and you do not die from the disease. It's a progressive disease, meaning the symptoms get worse over the life of the disease.

I could tell many more stories, both good and bad, about the way children have reacted to my body's movements. Instead, I will simply ask those of you who are parents to share with your children the importance of accepting people who might be different. Explain that just because somebody walks or talks in a different way, or shakes, or is in a wheelchair, he or she is still God's child, and they shouldn't stare or make fun.

There's a group of kids who follow me out of basketball games, and they point and laugh at me all the way to my car. I usually ignore them, and I always pray that they will be forgiven. But, as the title of this book indicates, when I get to heaven, I won't be shaking anymore. My soul is tremor free.

MY NAME IS SPECIAL AGENT JACKSON

I love my job. I find it exciting to unravel the tangled web of deception that was assembled by the "bad guy." I have been blessed to have worked with some outstanding agents and for some excellent supervisors.

But a large percentage of PD victims lose their jobs. And that can sometimes lead to losing your family. This is one reason to arm yourself with the Word of God and surround yourself with fellow Christians. They will love you for who you are. Because Christians "know how the story ends," we don't fret earthly trials.

I praise God that my supervisors at the IRS have been supportive of me. They've been there every step of the way, providing me with encouragement. I believe I have earned the right to retire based upon my work ethic. Thousands of other PD patients have earned that right, also, but have been brushed aside, forced to retire or quit. Fight to keep your job if you believe you can still do it well.

TIDBITS

I suggest that you not attempt to hide your condition from your employer. I included my supervisor in all my medical updates. If you don't include him in your battle, this deception will ultimately surface, and your employer will wonder what else you didn't tell him.

Besides, the patient is often not the first one to notice a change. Your employer might be expecting news from you due to a symptom that you may have ignored.

My work group in Memphis has greatly assisted me in battling PD. We are a diverse group in gender and race, but we are connected by the job we do and a love for one another. Over the past eight years each of them has been instrumental in my life. The women have kept an eye on me, watching to see if I looked a little tired and weak, or if I needed a chair, some water, or just a hug. That's one thing our group does plenty of: hug!

I am grateful for my Memphis "family," especially Blanche, Andre, John, Kim, Donna, Alice, Robert, Tom, Debbie, Teressa, Sue, Shari, Marguerite, and Brad. I'm certain that our merciful and mighty Lord is preparing a special place in heaven for each of them.

Not all of my fellow agents are Christians. But Brad is a brother in Christ, and he and I share many similarities in our faith walk.

I hope you have someone like Brad in your life. He does everything 100 percent. When I first met him, he was a 100 percent sinner. We became close friends because we're both golfers.

When I Get to Heaven, the Only
One Shaking Will Be Elvis

Golf was something else that Brad did 100 percent. He played what I call "travel golf", that is, he played almost weekly in some sort of tournament so he could be measured against others. Travel golf can lead to problems because you're always at a party, which can lead to drinking or worse.

But when Brad became a born-again Christian, he gave the Lord 100 percent of his life. Now, I enjoyed the old Brad. But the new and improved Brad is my brother in Christ, and I will enjoy his company for eternity. He is truly a man of God, and I thank God for opening his eyes to the truth. His service to his church, through teaching, witnessing, and leadership, is a marvelous example of how to live a Christ-centered life. He has been a dear friend to me, always there to add a word of encouragement, a Bible verse, or just a hug to pick me up. I know God will continue to use him in powerful ways.

TIDBITS

The love of a spouse is unmatched, especially when that person is your primary caregiver. However, maintaining some of your "pre-Parkinson's" friends is also important. Nurture these friendships.

My friendships dwindled somewhat after I was diagnosed, but the ones that remained grew stronger. I know I have many close friends who will come if I need them at the drop of a hat. That knowledge is the source of endless comfort.

God only gave me one blood sister, but I think He made up for that by placing my partner, Kay Frye, in my life. Her friendship and support have meant the world to me.

If I ever felt as though PD was placing me, another agent, or anyone else in harm's way, I would retire immediately. Fortunately, God has blessed me with a slow-to-develop strain of PD, and I actually feel as though I am in better health today than I was two years ago.

I grieve for my brothers and sisters with PD who are not as fortunate as I have been. PD can be a vicious foe. But if you can meet it head-on, with the help of a mob of supporters, it doesn't stand a chance. Throw yourself into your faith and let God lead you to new victories.

TIDBITS

Exercise that includes light weights and stretching can give you better use of your muscles and reduce rigidity.

PLAY THE CARDS YOU'RE DEALT

PD can rob you of many things. It can take your speech, your independence, and your ability to walk or write. But it cannot touch your soul.

Jesus claimed my soul when He died on the cross for me. I accepted Him as my Lord and Savior and gave him my soul for safekeeping.

I wage a constant battle with the devil. He has tried wine, women, and song, as well as work, golf, and PD, to try to wrest my soul away from my Lord. But (in my worst Southern grammar) "it ain't gonna happen!" Yet I cannot totally forget my friend PD. It is with me every day.

When I Get to Heaven, the Only
One Shaking Will Be Elvis

Tom Watson played in the 2003 United States Open golf tournament. His game was outstanding, and it was dedicated to his lifelong caddie, Bruce Edwards. In January of 2003, Bruce was diagnosed with ALS, commonly called Lou Gehrig's disease.

Bruce's health deteriorated quickly. Yet he carried that big bag up those numerous golf holes with a smile on his face. In an interview following the tournament, Bruce said he had been truly blessed.

You must play the cards you are dealt; there are no re-deals in life. Bruce, like anybody with a serious illness, could have chosen to live out his life shut up as a hermit, waiting on death to knock at his door. But he didn't. He became an example of how to battle a disease.

Bruce Edwards died shortly after the 2003 golf season. He may have lost his personal battle with ALS, but I believe the attention that he and Tom Watson brought to this dreadful disease will help find a cure. Bruce died fighting his disease on his terms, never giving in to it or feeling sorry for himself. That is a life lesson for us all.

On the flip side is the life of a former friend of mine, whom I'll call John. John showed all the signs of being a Christian. He was at church every time the door opened, served as an officer in the church, and taught Sunday school. He was married to a wonderful lady and had two children.

When John was diagnosed with terminal cancer and given only months to live, he turned his back on the one Person who could have helped him through his journey. He became bitter toward God, openly cursing Him. He left his church, his wife, even his children, and died a lonely death.

Contrast that to my buddy Bill Cox. Bill is the "king of hugs." Every Sunday at Fellowship I receive a hug from Bill. But Bill shouldn't even be here to give me those hugs. Years ago, he went to the doctor's office and heard pretty much the same words John did—He had cancer and there was little hope he would live.

Bill went to the Lord in prayer, along with hundreds of his friends and family members. Many of Bill's friends asked other people to fast and pray for him as well.

Our awesome God answered those prayers. Bill remained strong in his faith. And even though he was supposed to have died more than fourteen years ago, he is alive and well today. He and his remarkable wife, Teresia, have two little girls, Rebekah and Jennie, who would not be on this earth if God had not answered those prayers.

Unlike John, Bill turned his troubles over to the one Person who could handle them—God.

Several friends have had me on their prayer lists for eight years now. Every time I go to my doctor's office in Atlanta, people fast and pray for me. What an extraordinary support group I have.

Like my brother in Christ Bill Cox, I have turned my worries about the future over to my God, who I know can handle them all.

TIDBITS

I wrote this book to assist others in coming to know God. He is my ultimate comforter, my confidant, my strength, and my shield. If you or a loved one has been diagnosed with PD, the first and most important step is to establish or strengthen your relationship with God. Get to know Him. Need strength? Feel like you can't take another step? Trust in our Savior, who will walk with you step by step, even carry you if needed, to the finish line, heaven, where all of your problems will be removed.

Mary & Denton Sims

My Mother Bettye Jackson

Charlie Schuchard & Denton Sims

In-laws—The Sims, Schuchards & My Family

Out-laws—My Mother, The Roberts & My Family

Special Agent Bill Cade, retired, my mentor

My best friends, the Dotsons, Laura, my wife, and me

Bob Kunze and me at the Master's

Michael, "100% Brad", Bill and me take on Bear Trace, Chickasaw

Chapter 3

FROM HERE TO ETERNITY

And above all, don't give up. Don't ever give up.
—Coach Jim Valvano[iv]

My faith walk started when I was a young boy. My father was not a church-going man. Jack Jackson was an alcoholic, plain and simple. I cannot remember a single day when he took us to church, although there must have been a time or two. My mother took me to church, although she usually didn't stay. She later told me that many times she didn't stay due to the marks of physical abuse that had been left by my father.

My precious mother has seen more than her share of heartache. I think I received my "never say die" attitude from her. She lost two brothers in World War II, was married to an abusive man, and battled cancer. She is a fighter. And she was always there for me.

When I Get to Heaven, the Only One Shaking Will Be Elvis

My sister, Celia, and her husband, Edwin, raised me. Edwin took me hunting and answered dozens of questions that a loving father would have. Celia has endured the loss of a child, yet still maintains a positive outlook. They have both been wonderful. I pray you have such a strong support group.

TIDBITS

Support groups that meet to share information on the disease and its treatment are very important for you and your caregiver. Seek out a group in your area. If you can't find one, start one yourself.

My support group begins with my wife and daughters and spreads out to Laura's family and mine, and then to my church, and finally to my friends from work. I am truly blessed to have all this support. It has made living this unique life a lot easier.

I am especially grateful for my nieces and nephews: Lisa, Mary Margaret, Scott R., Scott S., and Mike. I must also include my "little angel," my nephew Trip, who was killed in an automobile accident at the age of ten when a drunk driver ran his grandmother's car off the road. Trip was my first nephew and we were super close. Trip is in heaven now, and I look forward to spending eternity with him.

Tidbits

Approximately 10 percent of patients diagnosed with PD are between the ages of twenty-one and forty.[v] If you fall into this "young onset" category, pay close attention to your mental health. Seek the help of a mental health specialist. And don't forget God, who has broad shoulders.

Be Careful How You Dress in a Snowstorm

One year in West Tennessee we had a bad winter. One of the worst snows we had that year was about seven inches in one day.

I was having my usual sleepless night when the television announced that all of the schools were closed due to the snow. Being a considerate husband, I decided to sneak into my wife's room and take her dog out for a walk. Bear was a Schipperke that we inherited from my dad when he died. He was small, about eight pounds, and jet black.

Since I didn't plan on being out long, I stayed in my sleep clothes: boxers and a T-shirt. I had taken my medicine earlier and felt sure that it had kicked in. So out I went to walk Bear. The snow was coming down pretty hard.

I noticed the newspaper by the street, so I trekked out to get it. Just as I straightened from picking up the paper, PD hit me hard. I couldn't move, frozen in both body and mind.

When I Get to Heaven, the Only One Shaking Will Be Elvis

I heard my neighbor Phil Bradberry coming out to get his paper, but I was frozen, with my back to him. Phil said something about it being a lovely morning. I tried to let him know I needed help. But PD made my voice low and garbled.

I heard Phil walk away. I kept trying to yell, "Help!" But my frozen voice didn't reach very far.

So there we were. My black dog was covered with white snow. I had about two inches of snow on my head, and parts of my body felt like they were freezing off. Bear looked at me as if to say, "OK, we can go inside now." It must have taken a good fifteen minutes before I could shuffle in.

Many times over the years we had him, Bear made me laugh. He often tilted his head from side to side when PD made my steps awkward, as if he was worried about me.

The day Bear died was a sad day in the Jackson household. That dog occupied a special place in my heart, a place that was once held by my prior dog, Annie. I hope I get to see my dogs in heaven. They have been loyal friends and I miss them.

TIDBITS

Pets can be good companions for Parkinson's patients. They give unconditional love.

BE CAREFUL WHAT YOU PUT IN YOUR SHOPPING CART

When I look in the mirror I can still see that high school football star. Time sure does fly by.

I began my midlife crisis on my forty-ninth birthday. I was looking through the Sunday sales flyers when I noticed that Kmart had boxers on sale. And not just any boxers. These were Joe Boxer's American Flag boxers. I just had to have them.

So I climbed into my jeep and drove to Kmart. In the store, I began to notice that funny feeling that PD gives me right before it slaps me between the eyes. But I felt confident that this was a false signal because I had already medicated myself. I placed the boxers in my shopping cart and covered them with some envelopes that my wife needed.

PD often attacks my walk, but this time it added a new twist: the return of the tremor. Somehow I made it to the checkout stand, where an elderly woman was working the register. As she rang up my purchases, she held up the boxers for all to see and asked in a loud voice, "Are these yours, darlin'?"

When I started trembling, she looked concerned. I explained to her that I had Parkinson's Disease, and I asked if she would help me get to the chairs near the checkout stand, which she did. Thankfully, in a few minutes the medication kicked in and I was able to drive home.

Freezing, and the fear of it, was starting to control my life. I could never tell when it was coming on, but when it did, it came on quickly. I knew something had to be done. So I placed that near the top of my prayer list.

I don't worry about freezing much anymore.

YOU ARE WHAT YOU EAT

If you don't feel comfortable with your PD doctor, find a new one. You deserve the peace of mind that comes with being sure of your diagnosis and feeling comfortable with how your doctor plans to attack it.

Dr. Rowland sent me to a Parkinson's specialist in Memphis, Dr. Ronald Pfeiffer. Right from the first meeting I felt comfortable with him. He was confident in the way he attacked PD.

This relationship lasted almost six years. At that point my condition reached a level where Dr. Pfeiffer thought surgery might be in order. So I made an appointment with a doctor in Memphis. This doctor, a brain surgeon, had the bedside manners of Jack the Ripper. He burst into the room, gave me a quick exam, then asked me what I wanted. I explained that I was there to determine if I was a candidate for deep-brain stimulation, an operation where electrodes, placed into the brain, are stimulated by a pacemaker device implanted in your chest.

Well, "Dr. Personality" looked at me and said something like, "We can cut on you, but I just killed my sixth patient last week."

I ran out of that guy's office, and I never returned.

I still wanted to have the surgery, though. I was fine at work, but when the medication wore off, I was basically homebound.

Dr. Pfeiffer and I decided a second surgical opinion was in order. He contacted Emory University Neurology Department in Atlanta, Georgia. My mother had a friend whose son went there for treatment for his Parkinson's, and she had suggested Emory.

The Emory Clinic, part of the teaching hospital of Emory University, has a Movement Disorders office that assists patients with a variety of brain disorders, including PD. The Chief of Neurology at this clinic is Dr. Delong, a no-nonsense educator who knows what he's doing. His credentials are quite impressive. He's even Mohammad Ali's doctor.

I have no doubt that God put this great healer in my life. He has done wonders in my battle with PD. My visits with him have helped me reach a level of independence I didn't have in the first three or four years.

No other doctor ever made a link between my food selection and my symptoms. Dr. Delong determined that I was eating too much protein. He stated that I should have no more than seven grams each day. That's one piece of meat about the size of a deck of cards. At that point, I was eating a protein bar at 10:00 A.M., drinking a protein shake for lunch, topped off with another protein bar at 2:00 P.M. Total grams for my midday food intake: thirty-one! Dr. Delong said that if King Kong had PD and were ingesting that much protein, he would be shaking.

When I Get to Heaven, the Only
One Shaking Will Be Elvis

I curtailed the protein in my diet and the positive results have been incredible.

TIDBITS

To date, no special diets have been developed to slow the progression of PD. However, a diet that is high in protein has been shown to interfere with the effectiveness of the medicine levodopa. In my case, protein caused freezing.

One morning I was heading out to the golf driving range to hit some balls. I now knew that too much protein would mess me up. But my jeep, totally on its own, pulled into Latham's, a café that serves good food. I figured one sausage biscuit wouldn't hurt.

I drove to the range and parked at my usual place at the far end of the lot. My PD didn't zap me until I had hit almost the entire bucket of balls. As I felt the freezing coming on, I was able to make it to the bench that I had pulled up behind my post.

The young men inside the pro shop, thinking nobody was on the range, turned on the sprinklers. Now, golf course sprinklers put out a lot of water. I was quickly soaked, as was my new Ole Miss bag, and if I could have made it inside that building, those young men would have been soaked!

That episode was totally my fault. I knew what would happen if I ate protein, and I did it anyway. Color me *stupid*.

JOHN WAYNE IS STILL ALIVE

John Wayne will always be a member of my family. With no brother and no father figure, I learned about life from "Uncle John." He helped me through those awkward male formative years.

In the movie *The Searchers*, he taught me about commitment and persistence. In *The Quiet Man*, he taught me about standing up for your beliefs. In *The Shootist*, he taught me how to die on your own terms.

God has put a lot of "John Waynes" in my life. When I was struggling about whether to drop out of college, He sent me a brother-in-law who showed me the right way to live. When I married, God gave me a superb father-in-law to teach me how to be a family man. Over the years, whenever times of struggle have come into my life, God has introduced new friends.

One such friend is Bill Cade, who helped bring me to the foot of the cross. Bill is truly a man of God. He and I were partners in the Jackson office for more than ten years. He taught me, through both words and actions, the importance of having God in your everyday life.

God has always placed special people in my life before something dreadful happens to me. I have actually become rather apprehensive. With all the Christian men He has provided in Fellowship Bible Church, I can't imagine what's going to happen next!

I hope God has supplied you with "John Waynes" in your life.

TIDBITS

Here are some ways you can make dressing yourself easier.

a. Wear shoes that are easy to get on and off. Sandals, flip-flops, slip-ons, or shoes with Velcro are much easier than ones that tie.
b. Find clothes that don't require buttons. And get ties that clip on. (But watch out for the fashion police!)
c. Suspenders are easier than a belt.
d. Boxers are preferred over briefs. (Not really; I just wanted to see if you were paying attention.)

MISTAKES, I'VE MADE A FEW, BUT THEN AGAIN, TOO FEW TO MENTION

My apologies to Mr. Sinatra for borrowing a line from one of his songs. But I have made mistakes. However, unlike the song lyrics, I have made many. I will mention several here that I hope you won't have to make.

The first mistake that comes to mind happened soon after I was diagnosed with Parkinson's. I gave up one of my hobbies.

I had been an athlete all my life. I guess my father gave me a competitive spirit. In seventh grade I told him I wanted to go out for football. He asked me why, and I just told him I loved it. The only thing I remember him telling me was that if I went out for the sport, I could not quit.

He must have been a prophet, because as soon as I found out how hot a Mississippi August can be when you're dressed in a football uniform, I asked if I could quit. Of course he said no. I begged him to let me quit. He still said no.

About two weeks later, after I got into shape, I was fine. I started at offensive and defensive tackle that year.

My athletic ability carried me through high school, where I lettered multiple times in every sport, and on to junior college, where I played football and baseball. After college, I turned to golf. When I wasn't playing, I could often be found practicing at the course or range. After Laura and I got married, I still played or practiced almost every day.

But soon after I was diagnosed with Parkinson's, I turned my back on this part of my life. What a mistake!

Friend, do not give up anything for Parkinson's disease.

I have recently begun to play again. I hope I never let golf consume my every thought, as I once did. Just making it part of my battle against PD is victory enough.

My friend Bob Kunze has refused to let me give up the game. Bob would drive from Dallas, Texas, to Jackson, Tennessee, about a nine-hour drive, just to make me dust off the clubs and play. I hope you have a "Bob" in your life who will drag you kicking and screaming into your new life with PD.

When I Get to Heaven, the Only
One Shaking Will Be Elvis

Bob has never expressed pity for me, at least not in my presence. But I remember one golf tournament when tears welled up in his eyes as he watched me attempt to swing, but was shaking so bad that I couldn't. I also remember the pride on his face when, later in that very game, I drove the green on a Par 4 and we made the eagle putt to win our flight. I look forward to spending eternity on the fairways of heaven with this dear friend.

Bob came to my house one day in the spring of 2004, and we had several long talks about my faith. Bob also had talks with Jerry, Brad, and some other Christian friends of mine. He went home with a tape series from my church on faith. I also asked him to read an early manuscript of this book you're now reading.

A few days later Bob called, saying he wanted to accept Christ into his life. He's now on fire for the Lord. Praise God!

A second mistake I made was giving up part of my social life. Now, I've never been a party animal. Actually, I am basically shy. So when PD came into my life, I sometimes used it to my advantage. Whenever I was invited to a party I didn't want to go to, I'd dust off my old friend PD and use him as an excuse not to go. But all that did was rob me of the pleasure of other people's company.

We PD patients must strive to give up our fear that everybody is looking at us. The truth is, most people could care less about you.

One more warning: If you send your spouse out to enough of these events without you, she/he might not come back one time. And if your spouse decides not to go because of you, this might cause hard feelings. Don't do things that will make your spouse unhappy. Be fair. Go ahead and beg off some of the parties, but not all of them. Jesus wants your light to shine to the nonbelievers who may be there.

A minister once told me that Jesus blessed me with Parkinson's, not because He wanted to see how I would handle it, because He already knew that. Jesus wants me to show others how to handle it.

Lots of people have asked me how I can be so positive. I always tell them, "Because I know how the story ends." Someday I will be in heaven, with my crown of righteousness, where only Elvis will be shaking.

Do not give up something you love because of PD. Ride a bike, swim, walk, or volunteer at a school. The disease may affect you in ways that will make some pleasures almost impossible. But do what you can to the best of your abilities. Perhaps you can only play a few holes of golf. That's better than none. You may need to ask a friend to help. That's OK. Just don't give everything to PD. Fight it every step of the way.

A SECOND HELPING OF MY FAMILY

My daughter Sims is now almost seventeen. She is an accomplished soccer player and a natural driver. She hides her tender heart well, but I know it is there. Several people have told me that Sims has asked them to pray for my health. She is a special young lady and I praise

God for her. If there is justice in this world, Sims will have a child just like her someday.

Mary Elizabeth is almost nineteen. She attends Ole Miss, were she is an artist, singer, and all American shopper. She is very independent, and we joke that as long as we keep sending money she may never come home.

Both girls are very helpful when I need them. I hate that they have to help me, but they don't seem to mind.

Laura is the rock in this family. She expects me to pull my weight around the house, PD or not. She is my caregiver, friend, lover, wife, and mother of my children. That's a lot of hats to juggle. And she does so with grace.

FINAL UPDATE

As of this writing, I am weeks away from retiring. While I prepare to close the book on my career as a special agent, I find myself somewhat apprehensive about what's next in my life. I intend to write additional books. Currently, I have six projects at various stages of completion. Everyone who loves to write dreams of being a success. This book has already been a success because, in a small way, it helped my friend Bob become a Christian.

I am battling a mighty foe. One that never sleeps, rests, or takes holidays. But I have marvelous support, both from my family and from my church.

So, what's next for me? I don't have a clue. But I will meet whatever it is head-on, with help from my three F's: Faith, Family, and Friends.

LADIES AND GENTLEMEN, ELVIS HAS LEFT THE BUILDING

I believe I have a long life ahead of me as I continue the battle against my constant companion, PD. I intend to fight it every step of the way with prayer, medicine, and laughter.

Whatever your health problem is, I recommend that you have the following in place:

a. A strong faith in God. This faith needs to be biblically based and must include regular prayer.

b. Strong support groups, beginning with your family and branching out to your church and work associates. Nurture these relationships. Share with these people your successes as well as your concerns. Let them into your life; don't shut them out.

c. A doctor you feel comfortable with and can talk to candidly. But remember, PD treats everyone a little bit differently. No two cases are exactly the same. So have patience. If necessary, seek a second opinion. There might be another doctor who has the right plan for you.

    d.   Do not give up your hobbies.

    e.   Be an example of how to conduct oneself in public. Exhibit your best manners and a positive attitude.

    f.   Bring laughter into the battle. I laugh every day about something that PD does to me. Every day with laughter is a day that you beat Parkinson's.

I want to leave you with some words of wisdom from the late Coach Jim Volvano, who won a national basketball championship as head coach at North Carolina State. While I never had the pleasure of knowing "Coach V," I feel as though we are brothers, fighting the despair and depression that come when you battle disease. Coach Valvano died of cancer after a short but courageous battle with that wretched disease. In a speech he made at the ESPY Awards, where he was presented the Arthur Ashe Award, Coach Valvano said, "To me, there are three things we should all do every day of our lives. Number one is laugh. Number two is think. And number three is, you should have your emotions moved to tears—could be happiness or joy."[vi]

What a powerful message "Coach V" left behind for others to share and learn from. I would add my personal challenge to all PD patients and their caregivers to accomplish these same three things.

    a.   Laugh—at yourself, at PD, at something that has happened in your life. Laughter is great therapy for you and good medicine for those who are watching you.

b. Think. Don't let PD rob you of your ability to use your brain. Consider what you can do to make each day as normal as possible. Be a vital member of your family, your church, and your community.

c. Cry. Tears are healthy. But don't cry about what you can no longer do. That will tarnish all the precious memories of the things you did and all the hope for the things you can still do. I cried a little the other day when my wife asked me if I was going to take my younger daughter on a father-daughter white-water rafting trip. I would love to, but it will probably not be possible. PD might win some of these battles, but I won't let it win the war.

Following is a Bible passage that I hope will comfort you as you fight this disease.

> For I am already being poured out like a drink of-fering, and the time has come for my departure. I have fought the good fight, I have finished the race, I have kept the faith. Now there is in store for me the crown of righteousness, which the Lord, the righteous Judge, will award to me on that day.
> —2 Timothy 4:6-8

Fight the good fight, finish the race, and above all, keep the faith. Because what waits for you is the crown of righteousness and the sword of salvation. May God pour His endless blessings over you, and may His grace grant you peace.

ENDNOTES

[i] Paul Nausieda, M.D. and Gloria Bock, M.S.N., R.N., C.S, *Parkinson's Disease: What You and Your Family Should Know* (Miami, FL: National Parkinson Foundation, Inc.,1999), p. 7.

[ii] American Parkinson's Disease Association pamphlet.

[iii] Nausieda, *Parkinson's Disease,* p. 47.

[iv] http://www.americanrhetoric.com/speeches jimvalvanoespyaward.htm.

[v] Paul Nausieda, *Parkinson's Disease,* p. 46

[vi] http://www.americanrhetoric.com

CONTACT INFORMATION

To order additional copies of this book, please visit
www.redemption-press.com.
Also available on Amazon.com and BarnesandNoble.com
Or by calling toll free 1-844-2REDEEM.

CPSIA information can be obtained
at www.ICGtesting.com
Printed in the USA
LVHW01s2351261017
553968LV00016B/525/P